Twenty-Five Security User Stories for Secure Agile Development

By

Stephen M. Dye

DEDICATION
This book is dedicated to my Loving Mother, Patricia Dye 1932-2014.

This page left intentionally blank

FOREWORD

Software development and security have long been perceived as contrary disciplines. Software development is about functionality, features, usability, defined requirements, tangible milestones, and most recently, has become an engine of economic and cultural growth worldwide. Security, on the other hand, is often viewed as the opposite of these things: non-functional, obtrusive, poorly defined, and potentially the wrench in the gears of the aforementioned engine of growth.

The ongoing evolution of software development methodologies towards increasingly rapid release cycles has only deepened this perceived tension. The set of development methods known as Agile exemplify this trend, with their focus on speed, iteration, lightweight processes, and continuous change. When I first heard of Agile, I immediately recoiled. I'm one of those uncool security guys, and I despaired that getting developers to pay heed to security was hard enough already without fanning the flames. After finally starting to feel welcome at the table of software development, security suddenly seemed doomed again to irrelevance in the software sphere.

Gradually, as Agile itself evolved, security and dev began to find common ground again. Security practitioners began to adapt to this new paradigm, learned the lingo (stories, backlog), and as I write this, seem on the verge of realizing that there might even be benefits to iterative, rapid change (see, for example, the exchange between security legend Marcus Ranum and veteran security leader Jim Routh about Agile and DevOps: http://goo.gl/QSrIJc).

The book you hold in your hands (or in your e-reader) is a powerful and practical contribution to the further alignment of Agile development and security. I've known Stephen for a number of years, and have firsthand experience with his passion and knowledge on the topic of software security from the practitioner's perspective—both development *and* security. Leveraging his considerable experience, he's compiled a very useful set of templates, examples, and guidance around that most important of Agile artifacts, the user story. Deftly, he's illustrated how this functionally focused development tool can be used synergistically to drive non-functional security properties into software development.

As many software security experts (including me!) would agree, the path to more-secure software begins with a threat model, and integrating security into user stories continues this time-honored tradition, now adapted to Agile development. In addition, Stephen has diligently documented the various security testing options for each security user story. This book is an all-around efficiency enhancer for scrum masters, product owners, development team members, and software security professionals. If you're an Agile shop, this is an invaluable toolkit for ensuring security is built in from the start, with maximum efficiency, which is a sure differentiator in the increasingly crowded software marketplace of today.

Joel Scambray, co-author of the Hacking Exposed series of books
Austin, TX
April 28, 2016

ACKNOWLEDGEMENTS

I'd like to thank the following people for their help and guidance in writing this book:

- Joel Scambray, Principal Security Evangelist, Cigital, Inc.
- BC Eydt, Founder and CTO, Pryvos Inc.
- Paco Hope, Principal Security Evangelist, Cigital, Inc.
- Mike Lyman, Senior Consultant, Cigital, Inc.

Introduction

This book sets out to equip Agile software development teams and security stakeholders with the tools needed to harden a software product by preventing the top 25 known software security bugs from appearing in its code. Whereas software security is very easy to read about, discuss, politicize, and debate, implementing it is the real challenge, and where the real work and thinking take place. Though it is easy to know what the SANS Top 25 or the OWASP Top 10 vulnerabilities are, building security in and making it an integral part of the software development life cycle (SDLC) is very much a challenge for any software and product development team. This book helps Agile teams implement the much-needed security that should be present in all software.

Typically, a software development team will focus on features and functions brought about by requirements or user stories, but have less regard for the nonfunctional requirements that bring us security. In the Agile development environment, favored by many and increasingly commonplace, the aforementioned features and functions are demonstrated to, and experienced by stakeholders, sponsors, and business owners at the end of a sprint. Therefore, the security aspects, unless specifically demanded, are *not* demonstrated by the development teams to anyone, including the security stakeholders.

The majority of software development teams do not focus on the security of an app; time, money, competing features, and the need for constant releases are treated as the priority items. Since money is usually a factor, the matter of security is further exacerbated by attempts to reduce the cost of labor by using very cheap, unqualified and undisciplined developers. The latter has the unfortunate effect of allowing insecure software to be developed, including permitting bugs and "undocumented features" to be built into the product, which is the exact opposite of what is truly required.

This book takes Agile teams through the process of building security into a software product. Traditional Agile team members are given additional security roles and responsibilities, and Agile supports the flexibility needed for these additional roles. The worksheets and tables provided at the end of the book serve to support scrum masters and product owners as they transition to their new, added responsibilities.

Contents

About this book 11

    What this book is 11

    What this book is not 11

How this book is organized 12

The challenge of software security 12

Composition of security user stories 13

Code testing 16

    Manual analysis 16

    Automated static analysis 17

    Dynamic analysis 17

    Functional analysis test 18

Agile team secure software responsibilities 19

    The scrum master 19

    The product owner 19

    The development team 20

Security Backlog Grooming 22

Security Sprints 22

Twenty-five security user stories 24

    SQL Command injection 25

    OS Command Injection 26

    Cross-site Scripting 27

    Dangerous File upload 28

    CSRF 29

    Open Redirect 30

    Classic Buffer overflow 31

    Path Traversal 32

    Download integrity Check 33

    Untrusted Control Sphere 34

    Dangerous Function 35

    Buffer Size 36

    Uncontrolled Format String 37

    Integer Overflow / Wraparound 38

Critical Function Authentication...39

Missing Authorization...40

Hard Coded Credentials..41

Sensitive Data Encryption...42

Untrusted Inputs: Security Decision..43

Unnecessary Privileges...44

Incorrect Authorization..45

Critical Resource..46

Risky Cryptography..47

Authentication Attempts..48

One-way Hash Salt...49

Tables for use in your organization...50

Mapping of security user stories to organization ID..50

Security User Story Test & Acceptance Matrix..50

Security User Story Backlog Grooming...50

Story Points and Priority Assignment Worksheet..50

Registering, sign-up, and updates..55

Useful Resources..55

SANS Institute 55

MITRE..55

National Institute of Standards and Technology (NIST)..55

Open Web Application Security Project (OWASP)...56

About The Author 56

Figure 1: Security user story table layout and format. 13
Figure 2: Selecting relevant security user stories for each sprint..................................20
Figure 3: Scrum team security responsibilities 21
Figure 4: A groomed backlog of security and user stories..22

Table 1: SANS Top 25 to Security user story & organizational ID mapping. 51
Table 2: Security user story test & acceptance matrix. 52
Table 3: Security user stories- backlog grooming. 53
Table 4: Security user stories- backlog grooming: story points and priority assignment.........54

This page left intentionally blank

About this book

What this book is

This book helps to organize and prepare Agile teams to develop their software securely. It is a practical workbook that shows how 25 security requirements in the form of security user stories can be designed, built in, and tested for correct implementation in an Agile development environment. This book provides scrum masters, product owners, and development teams with the necessary know-how to ensure security has been built into a software product using the SANS Institute's 25 most dangerous software errors. With the direction this book gives, scrum masters will be in a strong position to oversee and manage the development of secure software. Both scrum masters and product owners will learn about the threats to software products and the vulnerabilities that exist. More importantly, they will learn how to ensure these threats are eradicated or mitigated during the secure software development cycle, and not just prior to a release date or indeed after the release.

This book is a workbook. It is a practical implementation guide for applying 25 security user stories while developing in an Agile environment. Checking that a developer has properly implemented a security control or requirement is very difficult. Using the information in each of the 25 tables featured in this book, the reader is able to understand how a SANS Top 25 security control can be viewed in Agile terms, how it can be tested for, and how it can be proven that it was implemented.

What this book is not

This book is not a "how-to-securely-code" guide. It will not show a developer what code to write to meet a particular security objective. Numerous, books, training courses, and websites are dedicated to this topic, so why would the world need more on the subject? This book is also not a "how-to-pen-test" book, nor is it a tools book. Again, there are plenty of resources available to provide this guidance and wisdom.

This book does not claim that there are only 25 security risks in software worth considering; there are literally hundreds, but the ones in this book are the most notable at the time of writing. This book also does not assert that each software product will need to be developed with all 25 vulnerabilities in mind; this is certainly not the case, and as the reader progresses through the book, it will become apparent that great flexibility exists regarding which security user stories to apply in each sprint.

In this book, there are no theories, guesses, opinions, or projections for our world's future. This book will not pit one development language against another. It also won't compare or promote vendors. Finally, this book is also not a "how-to-run-an-Agile-team" book. It does, however, explore Agile team management, and the additional roles and responsibilities Agile team members will take on for software security.

How this book is organized

This book comprises the following building blocks:

1. The challenge of software security—an introductory explanation.
2. Security user stories—how each security user story in this book is composed.
3. Code testing techniques for Agile development environments.
4. Agile team secure software responsibilities—the security roles of each team member.
5. Security sprints—assessing existing code in a security-only sprint.
6. Security user stories–the SANS Top 25 vulnerabilities in user story form.
7. A checklist to choose a sprint's relevant security user stories and to assist with grooming.
8. A checklist to be used and re-used to ensure controls have been implemented in each sprint.
9. Tables for mapping security user stories to an organizations' controls.

This book is written for the following team members who work in an Agile environment:

1. Security stakeholders.
2. Product owners.
3. Scrum masters.
4. Developers.
5. Testers for the development team.

At a minimum, the people listed above should read and absorb the contents of this book. If the organization is large enough to employ user experience and user interface designers, solution and security architects, business process owners, and quality assurance teams, these individuals should also read the book to understand how their work will be impacted by the addition of the 25, non-functional security features covered.

The challenge of software security

Why is it so difficult to make software secure? Paradoxically, security is a negative goal; to secure something, we must understand just how insecure it is, either by trying to break it ourselves or by figuring out how other people would. As an example, a simple user input field on a mobile or web app may require the user to enter their name or perhaps a phone number. The coding for this is simple. However, illicit input to these fields in the form of non-alphanumeric characters such as symbols and certain sequences of characters can render an app useless by making it crash. The crash could cause the app to reveal information that would allow an attacker to further penetrate the app or a website.

Securing software is very complex. To secure the app, the security teams have to think of all the potential negative consequences that could arise if someone enters illicit or invalid data in a user-input field, and what that input might be. There are, understandably, many negative consequences to entering incorrect data in a user-input field, but there are also an equal number of measures that can be taken to prevent this. Naturally, there is a downside to the work needed to design and build countermeasures to these potential attacks. The extra thinking and planning lengthen the overall development and testing time the app will require, which is more negativity to think about!

Though a challenge, software security must not be ignored. Agile development, as the name suggests, is flexible and can accommodate the need for security. This book shows that applying, adding, inserting, or layering in security to new or existing code can be done through application of the security user story.

Composition of security user stories

Each of the 25 security user stories in this book consists of multiple building blocks designed to assist each member of the Agile product, management, and development teams. In this book, all security user stories are formatted and displayed as follows:

Security User Story ID # XXX	Vulnerability	Secure Agile
Priority:	Story Points:	
As a:		
I want:		
So that:		
Test Steps and Acceptance Criteria		
Manual Analysis. Automated Analysis. Dynamic Analysis. Functional Analysis. *Acceptance Criteria:*		
Independent ☒ Negotiable ☒ Valuable ☒ Estimable ☒ Small ☒ Testable ☒		
Definition of done:		
Definition of done achieved. ☐		

Figure 1: Security user story table layout and format.

Each individual component of the above table will be explored in detail, as described below:

1. **Security User Story ID # XXX (001 to 025):** Each user story is assigned an ID number for the purpose of tracking and identification. This number can be changed in accordance with the organization's scheme used for identification of user stories or security controls etc. The workbook tables, located towards the end of this book, allow the scrum master or project owner to map between the user story IDs in this book and the organizations' IDs.

2. **Vulnerability:** The name of the vulnerability refers to each one of SANS Top 25 vulnerabilities. Please use the table of contents to locate the exact page where each vulnerability appears. The electronic version of this book has hyperlinks for each vulnerability to assist the reader with navigation.

3. **Priority:** This is the priority that a product owner should give to a security user story to ensure correct prioritization for the sprint it is in. The initial value of 1 was assigned to permit easier sprint planning, since security user stories are a new concept. The workbook tables, located towards the end of this book allow the product owner to assign a priority value on blank worksheets for any security user story.

4. **Story Points:** In Agile development, each user story is assigned a story point, which indicates its relative importance. The same applies to security user stories to help Agile teams and leadership understand the severity of the breach that may result should the security user story not be implemented. Story points are typically assigned a value on the Fibonacci scale of 1,2,3,5,8,13, or 21. These are set to an initial value of 1 to permit easier sprint planning, since security user stories are a new concept. Once the value and need for security user stories are appreciated, the story point values can be adjusted according to the experience the team has gained from coding security in. The workbook tables, located towards the end of this book allow the product owner to assign story points on blank worksheets for any security user story.

5. **"As a_____, I want to_____, so that____"**: Traditional requirements are known as user stories in Agile. The *"As a__, I want to_, so that_"* form of expression provides Agile teams with the exact information required to understand how a security user story is used, why it is needed, and who it benefits. User stories look at the user experience and functionality required for the app to work correctly. This book looks at security user stories in the same manner: by expressing the secure experience and thus the necessary functionality required for the app to operate securely. An example is provided below. In this particular case, the need for protecting a users' credentials from brute force attacks is expressed as a security user story as follows:

> **As a:** *website or app user, stakeholder or data owner,*
> **I want:** *to prevent attackers from pre-computing hash values of passwords.*
> **So that:** *attackers can be prevented from bypassing any protection mechanisms lacking salt that would allow them to gain privileges using brute force and rainbow table attack methods.*

6. **Test Steps:** To assess whether the security user story has been implemented and is present in the code, tests should be performed prior to the end of the sprint. There are many ways to test and to determine if the security user stories are coded in. Though this book is not written to educate readers on software testing, a simple explanation of the methods used can help readers understand how the content is organized:
   a. **Manual analysis:** A manual code analysis employs a subject matter expert, capable of reviewing static code and spotting bugs in the programming. Manual code reviews often detect coding errors that an automated test may miss. Further information is featured in the "Code Testing" section.
   b. **Automated analysis:** An automated analysis uses software tools and can run through code at great speed, producing a report of the findings in a short space of time. For the purposes of this book, an automated analysis is an automatic static code analysis, and we are only concerned with the source code that has been written and/or obtained by the development team. Further information is featured in the "Code Testing" section.
   c. **Dynamic analysis:** A dynamic code analysis employs tools to automate tests on executing code, and is used to simulate multiple, iterative, and highly repetitive security tests. Further information is featured in the "Code Testing" section.
   d. **Functional analysis:** A functional analysis permits a tester to assess the app when running on a mobile device or web server in exactly the same way a real user would experience the app. Further information is featured in the "Code Testing" section.

7. **Acceptance Criteria:** The acceptance criteria are security features the app will possess if the security user story has been properly coded. In the Agile development environment, testers, scrum masters, and product owners are required to prove to security stakeholders that steps were taken to ensure security was coded into the app. The acceptance criteria form a useful checklist that allows the product owner, in conjunction with the testers and developers, to document that the pertinent security user stories are built in. An example acceptance criteria list is captured below:

> *The code:*
> *1.   Will generate a random salt on each occasion a new password is administered.*
> *2.   Adds the salt to the plaintext password before hashing it.*
> *3.   Generates a different salt for each password generation procedure.*
> *4.   Uses a strong, standard hashing algorithm.*

8. **Independent, Negotiable, Valuable, Estimable, Small, Testable**
   The INVEST mnemonic, made from the above six words, is used in Agile to describe how a user story is to be prioritized:
   a. **Independent** refers to how independent the user story is from others; some user stories depend on others to be developed first. This measure enables Agile users to prioritize user stories by putting independent ones first.
   b. **Negotiable.** User stories are the result of understanding, compromise, and agreement. They start out as a requirement or a user need, and are negotiated and optimized by the Agile team and the customer to become a user story. Whereas it is tempting to make a security user story non-negotiable, it is sometimes difficult to fully implement one when time, risk, and budget are factors. The security user story must, therefore, be negotiable, but every effort must be made to build security in still.
   c. **Valuable.** A security user story should, by definition, always have value, as it promotes security. However, we must consider practicality and applicability. As an example, there is no point in checking for buffer overflow vulnerabilities if the app is written in Java. On the other hand, the security user story has high value if the app is written in C or C++.
   d. **Estimable.** The security user story must possess the ability to be estimated in terms of level of effort required for implementation. This is so that it can be prioritized properly and the team knows how long it will need to re-code or code from scratch, and then test.
   e. **Small.** In an ideal Agile world, sprints should last no more than two weeks. Thus, security user stories should be small enough to allow several to fit in a sprint.
   f. **Testable.** To meet the acceptance criteria in (7) above, as well as to satisfy the "definition of done" in (9) below, the security user story must be tested. Therefore, in order for stakeholders to see that it was properly coded and implemented, it must be testable.

9. **Definition of done:** The definition of done is a final check-off, but more importantly, a sign-off by the product owner and scrum master to show the security user story was properly coded in, as proven by the security testing. The definition of done statement is used to inform all security stakeholders the app is ready for progression to the next stage in the lifecycle, which can mean release. An example of a definition of done statement is:

> *The app generates random salts for each new password that's added to the plaintext password, that uses a strong hashing algorithm, and the app did not crash or freeze during the tests.*

10. **Definition of done achieved:** This is simply a check box for the product owner to indicate the definition of done was achieved.

Code testing

This book is not a "how-to guide" on code testing, but it is worthwhile discussing the various methods of testing code to assist readers who are new to secure development. The software security industry typically groups code testing into three categories:

> 1. Static Application Security Testing (SAST).
> 2. Dynamic Application Security Testing (DAST).
> 3. Interactive Application Security Testing (IAST).

- **SAST** assesses code while in a static, non-executing state and is achieved through either manual or automated techniques, and looks at the app from an "inside-out" perspective.
- **DAST** assesses an app while the code executes, and looks at the app from an "outside-in" perspective, assessing what externally-viewable vulnerabilities may exist.
- **IAST** is an emerging technology that is essentially a combination of the above-two techniques, and is outside the scope of this book.

In this book, testing the code is recommended by performing the following types of analyses:

> **Static Application Security Testing (SAST).**
>
> 1. Manual code analysis.
> 2. Automated code analysis.
>
> **Dynamic Application Security Testing (DAST).**
>
> 3. Dynamic code analysis.
>
> **Optional, end-of sprint analysis and demonstration.**
> 4. Functional analysis.

Manual analysis

A manual analysis is essentially a *static analysis* of the code, conducted line-by-line by an expert in the field of code reviewing. A manual, static analysis can provide extremely accurate results with fewer false positives than a purely automated process. However, humans are fallible and cannot guarantee that they will catch all issues. Based on the quality of the reviewer, a manual static analysis may reveal many issues in the source code, such as cryptography errors, complex injection issues, potential problem areas with dead test code, and dormant code that is not executed.

One further aspect of a manual analysis's value is that it provides pin-pointed accuracy with regard to the location of a coding error; the line-by-line analysis will enable the expert reviewer to report exactly where the issue is located, which is not always possible with other types of analyses. Though a manual analysis, in some cases, is the most effective means of detecting some vulnerabilities, it does not detect vulnerabilities that may appear in the runtime environment. Thus, a combined static and dynamic test can be most effective.

Automated static analysis

An automated static analysis uses software tools to examine the code when it is static i.e., when the code is dormant and not executing. An automated static analysis is quick and has the advantage of producing a report with key findings in a short time. Automated analyses have the disadvantage of producing a number of false positives, i.e., they indicate an issue that in reality does not exist or, in some cases, cannot be replicated to the point of proving there was an issue. It is thus always recommended to triage the positive findings reported, identify false positives, and further investigate other positives to eliminate or label them as real. Key to an effective automated static analysis is knowledge of what actual tests the software tool is capable of carrying out. To test if the security user stories were implemented, the tester must be sure that the tool is able to detect the vulnerability being tested for.

The false positives generated from an automatic analysis could be a challenge for Agile teams, as time will be consumed performing the necessary triage to ensure all positives have been accounted for. Expertise is required to fully understand the false positives and determine if they are real issues or not. False positives are an unfortunate, yet a natural response to an automatic software scan; the tool does not understand the environment the application is designed to operate in, or how the app interacts with external systems, as it cannot trace the flow of data in the external system.

Similarly, a false negative can also occur: an error is missed and the tool is now overlooking a true vulnerability. This may occur because the most recent vulnerabilities for the app's environment are not known. Other possibilities stem from how the tool is configured or its inability to find the bug in question. If the scanning tool is only configured to look for a particular set of vulnerabilities, it could easily miss the intended coding weakness. To perform the tests in this book, Agile development teams should be well versed with a software tools' capabilities: what tests it can perform and how it can be configured, at a minimum.

Be aware that an automated static analysis may not be possible for all security user stories listed in this book. Such tools typically don't work with an app's context, i.e., they do not know what the app is supposed to do, whom it serves, and how it is used. These tools will only know if the developer has written incorrect code that makes the app vulnerable.

Dynamic analysis

A dynamic analysis works on executing code, and allows the tester to see exactly how the app behaves at runtime. The dynamic analysis also allows the tester to validate any findings made from a static code analysis if one has been performed. There are quite possibly many components such as libraries and databases or even peripherals that an app interacts with when running, and a dynamic analysis will assist in testing the code's security when interacting with these items. Testing in a runtime environment as opposed to the static, dormant environment, helps identify potential vulnerabilities which may have been missed in the static code analysis. A good dynamic test must be based on an equally good test plan. If a static analysis has been performed already, the results will assist in creating the test plan.

We must also consider the disadvantages of such testing. A dynamic analysis is an automated test, and automated tools, as has been seen, can produce false positives and skip the real issues, creating false negatives. As is the case with automated static testing, the capability of the dynamic analysis tool determines what tests can be carried out, and thus, whether a security user story's implementation can be tested.

Functional analysis test

The functional analysis is a useful means of testing some of the security abilities of an app and demonstrating them to security stakeholders at the end of a sprint. One example of a functional test is an attempt to enter an incorrect password and observe if the user is offered a chance to re-enter the correct password, or if the user is locked out after say three failed attempts. A tester can also assess and demonstrate the business logic, i.e., work through menus and options to assess if the app performs securely.

The analysis also offers the opportunity to attempt circumvention of security measures, without going to the depths a penetration test would. A functional analysis is optional during a sprint, unless time permits, but is really designed to demonstrate security to stakeholders at the end of each sprint or at the conclusion of a security sprint.

Agile team secure software responsibilities

Although this book is not about managing and building Agile teams, some guidance and suggestions on how to apply the security user stories in this book to a functioning Agile development team are warranted. Typically, an Agile team is composed of the scrum master, the product owner, and development team members- usually six people. Everyone has a role to play in Agile. The "security is everyone's responsibility" cliché/mantra also dictates that everyone in an Agile team should have both a security responsibility and a security role. The next three sections explore the security responsibilities and roles in the secure Agile team.

The scrum master

The scrum master's role is to ensure the development sprint stays on course and to attempt to prevent new features i.e. user stories being added during the sprint. In any sprint, adding new features to a software product is a major disruption. The same can be said for security user stories. Although Agile is capable of withstanding this to an extent, it is down to the scrum master to manage and ensure the sprint will be completed on time for user or security user stories. The scrum master should be fully aware that if another <u>functional</u> user story is inserted in the sprint unplanned, the corresponding <u>security</u> user stories must also be inserted; this will assist the scrum master in determining if the new <u>user</u> stories can be accommodated due to the need for the accompanying <u>security</u> user stories.

The scrum master must take advice and input from the product owner to ensure the security testers on the team are equipped with what they need in order to test each security user story. Tools and expertise are required to test for security, and the wrong tools, lack of tools, or deficiencies in team capability will impact both the sprint and the security of the software. The scrum master must also ensure the product owner selects applicable security user stories for the software being developed. A tool for doing this is illustrated in Figure 2.

The product owner

The product owner ensures the user stories to be built in the software are prioritized for inclusion in the sprints. In security terms, the product owner must ensure all pertinent user security stories from this book are selected for the software app in general and for the individual user stories. The product owner can use the tool illustrated in Figure 2 to assign relevant security user stories to sprints. A blank version of this tool appears in the latter part of the book, and is also available as a download for readers of this book who have become registered users. The product owner, just like a product manager, is responsible for the development and growth of the product, which must include its security posture. Just as a product possesses functional capabilities and features, it should also include the ability to withstand attacks from bad actors, and thus the implementation of the security user stories should be included in the product owners' responsibilities.

As a technical person, the product owner should provide support to the scrum master to ensure the development team has the right skills and tools in order to meet the time constraints of the sprint and the security goals of the product. As the reader should be aware by now, security user stories are no different from functional user stories; they require prioritization and assignment of story points to indicate their level of importance and relevance. Naturally, the product owner, who prioritizes security user stories, is also responsible for security user story backlog grooming, as well as managing the additional technical debt resulting from incorporating the security user stories. Figure 2 below shows how to assign relevant security user stories to sprints.

Security User Story Backlog Grooming																	
Scrum M:		Product Owner:	Sprint Number														
App:		Security Lead:															
ID#	Org ID#	Vulnerability	1	2	3	4	5	6	7	8	9	10	11	12	13	14
000	SEC-004	Example Vulnerability	X								X					
001		SQL Command injection	X			X										
002		OS Command Injection	X													
003		Cross-site Scripting				X										
004		Dangerous file upload	X													
005		CSRF		X												
006		Open Redirect	X													
007		Classic Buffer Overflow		X												
008		Path Traversal	X													
009		Download integrity Check		X												
010		Control Sphere	X													
011		Dangerous Function	X													
012		Buffer Size	X													
013		Format String	X													
014		Integer Overflow	X													
015		Critical Function Auth.	X													
016		Missing Authorization		X												X
017		Hard-coded Credentials	X													
018		Sensitive Data Encryption		X												
019		Untrusted Inputs		X												
020		Unnecessary Privileges		X		X							X			
021		Incorrect Authorization		X												
022		Critical Resource	X													
023		Risky Cryptography		X												
024		Authentication Attempts		X												
025		One-Way Hash Salt		X												

Figure 2: Selecting relevant security user stories for each sprint.

The development team

The development team in an Agile environment is charged with determining how and when features are built into the product. Each team is self-organizing and literally empowered to manage itself. Building security into the product should parallel the work done in building a user story. This is why security requirements have been made into security user stories. The difference between a standard and a secure Agile development team is that the latter must consist of secure developers and testers. The secure team will need developers who understand security and know when code is incorrectly written, as well as testers who can spot additional bugs and show the developers where the fix is needed. Therefore, the development team should consist of security-minded developers and testers who work side-by-side. Figure 3 on the next page summarizes the scrum team's security responsibilities.

Scrum Master Security Responsibilities

- Ensure all relevant security user stories are in all sprints
- Keep the sprints on track for secure, on-time completion
- Host a daily standup for secure coding progress
- Remove roadblocks to secure code writing and testing

Product Owner Security Responsibilities

- Groom security user stories to suit the user stories
- Identify and prioritize security user stories
- Ensure development team has the right SMEs and testing tools
- Support the scrum manager to meet the sprint's security goals
- Keep security stakeholders apprised of progress

Development Team Security Responsibilities

- Self organize according to secure coding needs
- Forecast secure coding and testing for the sprint
- Perform tests and immediately correct any bugs
- Report security progress to scrum manager daily
- Document all test results and outstanding issues
- Demonstrate security to security stakeholders

Figure 3: Scrum team security responsibilities

Security Backlog Grooming

As seen in Figure 3 above, the product owner and the development team are responsible for the backlog grooming. Once the product owner and team have groomed both the user stories and the security user stories, the output of the exercise is a series of prioritized, relevant, and ranked security user stories to accompany the sprints' user stories, as illustrated in Figure 4 below.

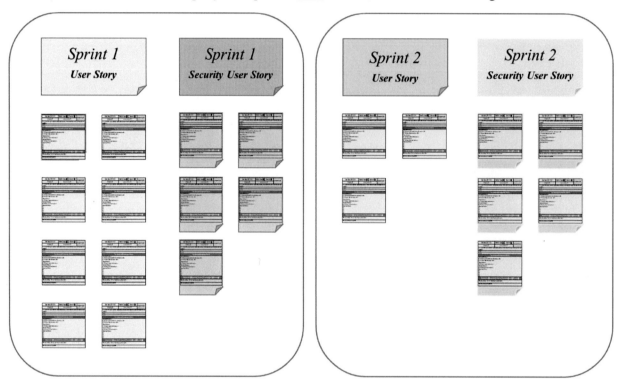

Figure 4: A groomed backlog of security and user stories

Security Sprints

Software security is best built in and not bolted on. In other words, as an integral part of software, security should be designed in and then coded in. Although security should not be an afterthought, what if that were the case with a certain product? It would not be the only app that did not have security designed in. How can security be layered into a software product when it was not done at the outset?

The security stakeholders and scrum team should explore integrating security into an existing product and achieve this through a *security sprint*. This security sprint would allow developers to modify existing code by studying each of the 25 security user stories and selecting those that are relevant and achievable. The product owner and development team should then determine the level of effort needed to incorporate each pertinent security user story in the security sprint.

This sprint, being dedicated to security only, must be properly planned, staffed, and equipped in order to meet its goals. This sprint will not be easy, but at the very least, it can demonstrate the advantages of building security in at the outset. To perform the security testing services, the Agile team could accomplish this internally, but also has other options as follows:

1. **Cloud-based software security assessment:** There are many cloud-based security service providers that accept customer's code, uploaded to their network. This code is automatically reviewed and a report created that indicates the areas of concern and where the issues exist. Though these services indicate areas of coding weakness and vulnerability, the scrum team should ensure the following is known before contracting with a vendor to provide the service:

   a. **What tests are carried out on the software**? Can testing of all SANS Top 25 vulnerabilities be conducted? The product owner should ask the vendor what standards or guides are used and whether the service providers can configure their tools to conduct SANS Top 25 and other custom tests.

   b. **What is the composition of the report?** Is it a highly technical report with all real and false positives containing automated comments only, or is it a groomed list of distinct problem areas with a professionally written, full report that the scrum manager, team, and product owner will understand? The scrum team should ask the vendor for a sample report to ensure they know exactly what they will receive and how it will be used. A hard-to-read, automatically-created report with results that need time to interpret may not advance the project any further.

   c. **Does the vendor provide a free retest?** Following a period allowed for remedying the software bugs, the vendor should offer a free retest to assess if the original bugs were fixed.

   d. **What is the Service Level Agreement (SLA)?** The length of the security sprint will be dependent on the speed at which the vendor can perform the tests, how quickly the development teams can fix any issues, and the time required for a retest.

2. **Integrated development environment (IDE) tools:** as an alternative, the development team could use an automated tool that reads code as it is being typed and entered in the development environment. These tools provide a real-time analysis of the source code as it is entered, showing weaknesses to the developers as they type. If this path is taken, ensure the tool vendor can prove that SANS Top 25 vulnerabilities are applied, and that the tool works with the particular language and platforms the organization uses beforehand.

3. **Professional and managed services:** as a final option, a third party could provide the security services through outsourced professional and managed services. This can be performed from a remote location or as on-site professional services.

   a. The **managed services** model utilizes live testers operating from a central location who use automated tools and conduct manual, eyes-on tests to analyze the code and produce the report. This service typically includes a 30-minute or longer briefing call to describe any findings. This service should also provide a free retest for any defects found that were subsequently corrected.

   b. The **professional services** model brings a live tester to the scrum team's organization who will use both automated tools and manual, eyes-on tests to perform the code review and produce the report. Naturally, the report will be manually created and briefed to the team in person. Such an engagement is typically time-boxed and based on a fixed fee. This service should also provide a free retest. An engagement featuring live testers who can provide a manually-written report, free of false positives, with an in-person briefing and a free retest, is well worth considering.

In order to work within the time and expense constraints of a security sprint, the professional services model can also be provided in the form of staff augmentation, where the tester(s) integrate with the development team and provide the code review services, knowledge transfer and general support for the duration of the project.

Twenty-five security user stories

The next 25 pages of this book are dedicated to the 25 security user stories that form the core of this book. Each page features a table as described in Figure 1, and refers to one of the SANS Top 25 security vulnerabilities at the time of writing. Each of the 25 vulnerabilities is accompanied by a set of recommended tests.

The type of tests chosen are based on their effectiveness in properly assessing the code for the particular vulnerability. This means that a manual analysis, for example, is only present when a manual analysis is deemed effective enough to not only test the code, but also warrant the level of effort needed to assess the code for the particular vulnerability in question.

In some cases, several types of testing are featured for each vulnerability e.g. manual, automatic and dynamic analysis. The product owner and scrum master should choose which tests to conduct in accordance with time and resource availability, but also the security goals of the sprint. Good planning and scheduling should allow all tests to be conducted which is the preferred option- particularly when a vulnerability requires a static and a dynamic test to be performed. This allows a pin-pointed spot check and run-time assessment to be performed, providing greater coverage.

Security User Story ID # 001	SQL Command injection	**Secure Agile**
Priority **2**	Story Points 1	

As a: **website or app user, stakeholder or data owner,**

I want: to protect all customer, user, product, and private information from being accessed, read, modified or erased by unauthorized users.

So that: the confidentiality, integrity and availability of the data are not compromised.

Test Steps and Acceptance Criteria

Manual Analysis.

(1) Perform a manual static code analysis to assess if the app contains a whitelist of acceptable input field characters and would reject such (but not limited to) inputs as:

- ' or '1'='1';
- ' or '1'='1' –
- ' or '1'='1' ({
- ' or '1'='1' /*

(2) Assess if the code generates error messages that contain information such as PII, credentials or app and system architecture.

Dynamic Analysis.

(3) Perform a dynamic analysis, executing multiple input fuzzing tests to attempt to simulate an attack on the app that would allow illicit access to the database.

(4) Assess if any error messages contain information such as PII, credentials or app and system information.

Functional Analysis.

(5) Enter numeric data e.g. "123" in alpha-only fields, alpha data e.g. "abc" in numeric-only fields, and random characters such as those in (1) above in any field and assess if:

- Entering the above and other illicit data to the input fields is rejected.
- Further access to the app or website is denied.
- The app crashes, freezes or otherwise acts in an unintended manner.

Acceptance Criteria:

1. The source code rejects illicit inputs as listed in the above items.
2. Any error messages generated do not contain PII, credentials or system information.
3. Functional and dynamic tests reveal further access is denied if illicit inputs are entered.
4. The app does not freeze or crash during the functional or dynamic tests.

Independent ☒ Negotiable ☒ Valuable ☒ Estimable ☒ Small ☒ Testable ☒

Definition of done: the tests have been carried out and the app rejected all incorrect/unwanted input, and the app did not crash or freeze during the tests.

Definition of done achieved ☐

Security User Story ID # 002	OS Command Injection	Secure Agile
Priority **2**	Story Points 1	

As a: website or app user, stakeholder or data owner,

I want: the app or a bad actor to not gain any privileges that allow the execution of dangerous commands directly on the operating system (OS).

So that: an unauthorized user or bad actor cannot gain access to the OS to achieve root-level privileges that will compromise the confidentiality, integrity, and availability of data.

Test Steps and Acceptance Criteria

Manual Analysis.

(1) Perform a manual static code analysis to assess the app's ability to restrict user privileges.

(2) Look for weaknesses that include a lack of input validation that would allow user input fields to be exploited as a means of injecting commands.

Functional Analysis.

(3) Perform a functional analysis by inputting data to form fields not relevant to the field such as numbers and special characters where only alphabetic characters are needed, and assess if the app rejects them.

(4) Attempt to inject a command that would enable an escalation of privilege or force the app to function outside of its intended sphere of operations.

Acceptance Criteria:

1. The app does not execute with privileges that allow access to the OS.
2. The app performs input validation on all form fields.
3. The app restricts user privileges and rejects command injection.

Independent ☒ Negotiable ☒ Valuable ☒ Estimable ☒ Small ☒ Testable ☒

Definition of done: the tests and analyses have been carried out, and it was proven that the app restricts user privileges, filters out command injection from any user input fields, and the app did not crash or freeze during the tests.

Definition of done achieved ☐

Security User Story ID # 003	Cross-site Scripting	**Secure Agile**
Priority **2**	Story Points 1	

As a: **website or app user, stakeholder or data owner,**
I want: **to prevent cross-site scripting attacks on a website or an HTML-based mobile app.**
So that: **users are not tricked into being re-directed to another website that will inject malicious code into their browser.**

Test Steps and Acceptance Criteria

Manual Analysis.
(1) Perform a manual static analysis to assess if there are any weaknesses or defects in the code that would lead to cross-site scripting (XSS) vulnerabilities.
(2) Ensure the analysis assesses all inputs to the app to trap illicit input such as arguments, query results, cookies, e-mail and anything read from the network, internet, and external systems.
(3) Assess if the code contains a whitelist of known good inputs that are relevant to the app only.

Acceptance Criteria:
1. The code contains a whitelist of acceptable inputs.
2. The app successfully detects and traps malicious input.
3. The code analysis shows the app exhibits no other cross-site scripting vulnerabilities.

Independent ☒ Negotiable ☒ Valuable ☒ Estimable ☒ Small ☒ Testable ☒

Definition of done: the tests and analyses have been carried out, and it was proven that the app can prevent cross-site scripting, and the app did not crash or freeze during the tests.

Definition of done achieved ☐

Security User Story ID # 004	Dangerous File upload	Secure Agile
Priority **2**	Story Points 1	

As a: **website or app user, stakeholder or data owner,**
I want: **to prevent malicious or accidental upload of potentially hazardous files.**
So that: **a device or system compromise resulting from the execution of malicious scripts and other actions can be prevented.**

Test Steps and Acceptance Criteria

Manual Analysis.

(1) Perform a static code analysis to assess if the app will allow a user to upload files of types other than what is allowed or required by the app.

(2) Assess if the code has any interpreters for script not required by the app.

Automated Analysis.

(3) Perform an automated static code analysis to assess if the app will allow a user to upload files of types other than what is allowed or required by the app.

Functional Analysis.

(4) If possible, carry out a functional test on the app and attempt to upload a series of executable, media, XML, and other types of files to assess if the app is able to accept or reject these files.

Acceptance Criteria:

1. The app successfully prevents the upload of files not required for operation of the app.
2. The app successfully prevents the upload of files that contain malicious script.
3. The app does not execute scripts not required for operation of the app.

Independent ☒ Negotiable ☒ Valuable ☒ Estimable ☒ Small ☒ Testable ☒

Definition of done: the tests and analyses have been carried out, and it was proven that the app can prevent the upload and execution of files not required for the operations of the app, those with malicious script in them, and the app did not crash or freeze during the tests.

Definition of done achieved ☐

Security User Story ID # 005	CSRF	**Secure Agile**
Priority **2**	Story Points **1**	

As a: **website or app user, stakeholder or data owner,**
I want: **to prevent cross site request forgery (CSRF) attacks.**
So that: **any requests to the website are verified as legitimately made by the user of the website.**

Test Steps and Acceptance Criteria

Dynamic Analysis.

(1) Perform a dynamic analysis preferably using a web application scanner and a fuzz tester to detect any weaknesses the code may possess.

(2) If possible, assess if the app accepts HTTP requests from an authenticated user and if it is unique to the user's session.

(3) Also assess if each link and form have unique tokens for each user.

Functional Analysis.

(4) Perform tests using the "OWASP CSRFTester" if possible, to identify any potential CSRF weaknesses.

Acceptance Criteria:

1. The dynamic test reveals all user session IDs are unique.
2. All links and forms have unique tokens for each authenticated user.

Independent ☒ Negotiable ☒ Valuable ☒ Estimable ☒ Small ☒ Testable ☒

Definition of done: the tests and analyses have been carried out, and it was proven that the app or website can prevent CSRF attacks, and the app did not crash or freeze during the tests.

Definition of done achieved ☐

Security User Story ID # 006	Open Redirect	Secure Agile
Priority **2**	Story Points 1	

As a: **website or app user, stakeholder or data owner,**
I want: **to prevent the user from being redirected to an untrusted or potentially malicious website.**
So that: **attacks that reveal personal credentials and other private data leading to a system or account compromise can be prevented.**

Test Steps and Acceptance Criteria

Manual Analysis.

(1) Perform a manual static code analysis to assess for source code weakness that would lead to an unwarranted URL re-direct.

(2) Ensure the code contains input validation and whitelists to screen out inputs that could potentially lead to a redirect.

(3) Also, ensure the code contains a warning banner or some form of notifying the user they are leaving the website and to where they are going.

Acceptance Criteria:

1. There are no source code weaknesses that would redirect a user to another URL other than that required for operations of the website.
2. Input validation and whitelisting are in place to prevent illicit input that would redirect a user.
3. Banners or warnings notify a user they are being directed to another page.

Independent ☒ Negotiable ☒ Valuable ☒ Estimable ☒ Small ☒ Testable ☒

Definition of done: the tests and analyses have been carried out, and it was proven that the website can prevent a redirect to another URL other than that required for operations of the website, and the app did not crash or freeze during the tests.

Definition of done achieved ☐

Security User Story ID # 007	Classic Buffer overflow	**Secure Agile**
Priority **2**	Story Points 1	

As a: **website or app user, stakeholder or data owner,**
I want: **to ensure that a buffer overflow condition does not occur.**
So that: **the arbitrary execution of malicious code, the app crashing, and the app entering a loop condition can be prevented.**

Test Steps and Acceptance Criteria

Automated Analysis.

(1) Perform an automated static code analysis and assess if any source code weaknesses exist that will cause a buffer overflow condition.

(2) Look for issues that do not consider stack buffer input size and any limiting.

Functional Analysis.

(3) Enter several, large numbers to input fields, and assess if the app is able to process them without crashing or freezing.

Acceptance Criteria:

1. The app considers: the range of inputs, potential results of processing various inputs and variables, and the size of the buffers that would be needed.

2. There are no source code weaknesses in the app that would cause a buffer overflow.

Independent ☒ Negotiable ☒ Valuable ☒ Estimable ☒ Small ☒ Testable ☒

Definition of done: the tests and analyses have been carried out, and it was proven that the app or website can prevent buffer overflow conditions, and the app did not crash or freeze during the tests.
Definition of done achieved ☐

Security User Story ID # 008	Path Traversal	Secure Agile
Priority **2**	Story Points 1	

As a: **website or app user, stakeholder or data owner,**
I want: **to prevent improper access to restricted directories through path traversal attacks.**
So that: **critical files required for the execution of apps or those that contain sensitive data cannot be removed, modified or exfiltrated.**

Test Steps and Acceptance Criteria

Manual Analysis.

(1) Perform a manual, static code analysis of the source code to detect the presence of any path traversal weaknesses in the code.

(2) Look for such weaknesses to include the inability to validate user input and suppress input that consists of such character sequences as: "../" or "/usr/local/bin."

Automated Analysis.

(3) Perform an automated, static code analysis of the source code to detect the presence of any path traversal weaknesses in the code.

(4) Look for such weaknesses to include the inability to validate user input and suppress input that consists of such character sequences as: "../" or "usr/local/bin."

Dynamic Analysis

(5) Perform a dynamic analysis of the source code to detect the presence of any path traversal weaknesses in the code.

(6) Utilize web app and services scanners to assess the app's ability to prevent illicit inputs.

(7) Use automated fuzzing techniques to attempt to traverse a directory path.

Functional Analysis.

(8) Perform a functional test by entering the sequences in (2) above, and any others that can be devised to assess the ability of the app to reject all illicit input attempts, and to assess it the tester can gain access to any network assets.

Acceptance Criteria:

1. The app performs input validation and filters illicit input.
2. The app rejects all attempts to traverse a directory path.

Independent ☒ Negotiable ☒ Valuable ☒ Estimable ☒ Small ☒ Testable ☒

Definition of done: the tests and analyses have been carried out, and it was proven that the website can prevent attempts at directory traversal, and the app did not crash or freeze during the tests.
Definition of done achieved ☐

Security User Story ID # 009	Download integrity Check	Secure Agile
Priority 2	Story Points 1	

As a: website or app user, stakeholder or data owner,

I want: the app to perform an integrity and origin check on any downloaded code.

So that: any downloads do not: come from unauthorized domains, have not been compromised while in-transit, and contain malicious code that would compromise the confidentiality, integrity or availability of any data the app uses or creates.

Test Steps and Acceptance Criteria

Manual Analysis.

(1) Perform a manual static analysis of the code to assess if the code implements detection and inspection mechanisms to identify any type of downloadable code- authorized, required or not.

(2) Assess if the app alerts users that unauthorized code or code that cannot be validated has been downloaded.

(3) Determine if the app detects any digital signatures on downloaded code and then validates them.

(4) Finally, assess if the code contains any interpreters that would execute code types not allowed or not required for the operation of the app.

Acceptance Criteria:

1. The app has detection and inspection mechanisms to identify any type of downloadable code- authorized, required or not.
2. The app alerts users that unauthorized code or code that cannot be validated has been downloaded.
3. The code detects and then validates digital signatures on any downloaded code.
4. The code does not contain interpreters that execute code types not required for the apps' operations.

Independent ☒ Negotiable ☒ Valuable ☒ Estimable ☒ Small ☒ Testable ☒

Definition of done: the tests and analyses have been carried out, and it was proven that the app can: prevent malicious code download, validate the integrity and origin of such code, alert the user or an administrator to malicious downloads and failed integrity checks, and the app did not crash or freeze during the tests.

Definition of done achieved ☐

Security User Story ID # 010	Untrusted Control Sphere	Secure Agile
Priority **2**	Story Points 1	

As a: **website or app user, stakeholder or data owner,**
I want: **the app to not import and execute code with malicious functionality from an untrusted entity, and to not contain any code or functionality unassociated with the app's purpose.**
So that: **privileges are not granted to external entities, third parties, and unauthorized users, and the app does not act in a malicious manner compromising data's confidentiality, integrity and availability.**

Test Steps and Acceptance Criteria

Manual Analysis.

(1) Conduct a manual static code analysis to understand if there are any hard-coded URLs and credentials or API calls that do not match the function of the app or hold the potential to be compromised which in turn, may cause an attacker to use these URLs or APIs as a proxy to attack the app.

Acceptance Criteria:

1. The app has no unnecessary libraries and code that do not match the function of the app.
2. The app contains no hardcoded URLs, credentials and API calls outside its intended function.

Independent ☒ Negotiable ☒ Valuable ☒ Estimable ☒ Small ☒ Testable ☒

Definition of done: the tests and analyses have been carried out, and it was proven that the app does not contain libraries, functionality, URLs, hardcoded credentials, and API calls outside the intended sphere of the apps' operations, and the app did not crash or freeze during the tests.

Definition of done achieved ☐

Security User Story ID # 011	Dangerous Function	Secure Agile
Priority **2**	Story Points 1	

As a: **website or app user, stakeholder or data owner,**
I want: **the app to use all APIs and function calls it requires in a secure manner.**
So that: **vulnerabilities with the potential to compromise the data's confidentiality, integrity and availability are not realized.**

Test Steps and Acceptance Criteria

Manual Analysis.

(1) Perform a manual static code analysis to assess for any source code weaknesses that reveal insecure ways of using APIs and functions needed for the intended function of the app, yet are not properly implemented.

Automated Analysis.

(2) Perform an automated static code analysis to assess for any source code weaknesses that reveal insecure ways of using APIs and functions needed for the intended purpose of the app, yet are not properly implemented.

Dynamic Analysis.

(3) Perform a dynamic analysis using a debugger to assess for source code weaknesses that reveal insecure ways of using APIs and functions.

Acceptance Criteria:

1. The code properly implements APIs and functions required for the app's intended purpose.

Independent ☒ Negotiable ☒ Valuable ☒ Estimable ☒ Small ☒ Testable ☒

Definition of done: the tests and analyses have been carried out, and it was proven that the app does not contain improperly implemented APIs and functions required for the app's purpose, and the app did not crash or freeze during the tests.

Definition of done achieved ☐

Security User Story ID # 0012	Buffer Size	Secure Agile
Priority **2**	Story Points 1	

As a: website or app user, stakeholder or data owner,
I want: to prevent the app from incorrectly calculating a buffer's size when allocating memory to it.
So that: the app will not crash, expose any sensitive data, or allow illicit arbitrary code to be executed.

Test Steps and Acceptance Criteria

Automated Analysis.

(1) Perform an automated static analysis and assess the code for any buffer overflow vulnerabilities.

(2) Ensure the test assesses the relevant sizes of the "from" buffer and the "to" buffer.

Acceptance Criteria:

1. The code properly calculates and is aware of buffer sizes, buffer contents, and intended content as a result of calculations, string manipulation etc.
2. The code allocates sufficient memory to buffers to assure the actions in (2) do not cause an overflow.

Independent ☒ Negotiable ☒ Valuable ☒ Estimable ☒ Small ☒ Testable ☒

Definition of done: the tests and analyses have been carried out, and it was proven that the app properly calculates and allocates memory to buffers, and the app did not crash or freeze during the tests.

Definition of done achieved ☐

Security User Story ID # 013	Uncontrolled Format String	Secure Agile
Priority **2**	Story Points 1	

As a: website or app user, stakeholder or data owner,

I want: the app to be invulnerable to format string errors in the "printf" style family of C/C++ functions.

So that: any illicit input from an attacker that can manipulate a format string which can cause buffer overflow and multiple other attacks resulting from inputted commands are prevented.

Test Steps and Acceptance Criteria

Manual Analysis.

(1) Perform a static code analysis and assess if the app is vulnerable to any of the following (but not limited to) table of untreated format functions:

a.	Fprint	b.	Vfprintf
c.	Print	d.	Vprintf
e.	Sprint	f.	Vsprintf
g.	Vsprint	h.	vsnprintf

Automated Analysis.

(2) Perform an automated static code analysis and assess if the app is vulnerable to any of the above (but not limited to) items in the table of untreated format functions:

Acceptance Criteria:

1. The app properly screens and rejects input for the above (but not limited to) table of format functions.

Independent☒ Negotiable☒ Valuable☒ Estimable☒ Small☒ Testable☒

Definition of done: the tests and analyses have been carried out, and it was proven that the app properly screens and rejects input for the above (but not limited to) table of format functions, and the app did not crash or freeze during the tests.

Definition of done achieved ☐

Security User Story ID # 014	Integer Overflow / Wraparound	Secure Agile
Priority **2**	Story Points 1	

As a: **website or app user, stakeholder or data owner,**

I want: **The app to prevent an integer overflow or wraparound when the app performs a calculation, for which the result will be larger than the original value.**

So that: **the app does not freeze, crash, enter an infinite loop, or execute any arbitrary code or commands.**

Test Steps and Acceptance Criteria

Automated Analysis.

(1) Perform an automated static test and assess the code for any integer overflow and wrap-around weaknesses and vulnerabilities.

Functional Analysis.

(2) Operate the app and attempt to enter large values, invalid input, and arbitrary code in an attempt to destabilize the app, make it freeze, crash, or respond in an incorrect manner.

Acceptance Criteria:

When tested with a wide range of input, the app does not:

1. Freeze or crash.
2. Become vulnerable to a denial of service attack.
3. Enter an infinite loop.
4. Enter conditions that would allow an attacker to execute any arbitrary code or commands.

Independent ☒ Negotiable ☒ Valuable ☒ Estimable ☒ Small ☒ Testable ☒

Definition of done: the tests and analyses have been carried out, and it was proven that the app properly handles integer input and is not subject to overflow and wraparound issues, and the app did not crash or freeze during the tests.

Definition of done achieved ☐

Security User Story ID # 015	Critical Function Authentication	**Secure Agile**
Priority **2**	Story Points 1	

As a: **website or app user, stakeholder or data owner,**
I want: **the app to challenge, authenticate and only then authorize users to access areas of the app that have specific functions, access sensitive information, and consume system resources.**
So that: **users- authorized or not, do not gain privileged access through unchallenged means to sensitive information, critical functionality and areas of the app or network that could lead to exposure, modification of sensitive information, or the injection of arbitrary code.**

Test Steps and Acceptance Criteria

Manual Analysis.

(1) Perform a manual static code analysis and assess the code for authentication presence or weaknesses.

Dynamic Analysis.

(2) If possible, perform a dynamic analysis, using a host application interface scanner to assess the code for authentication presence or weaknesses.

Functional Analysis.

(3) Attempt to navigate through the app and assess if there are any areas lacking authentication and authorization challenges.

Acceptance Criteria:

The app does not allow unchallenged access to areas:

1. Containing sensitive information.
2. Containing critical functionality.
3. That would allow the injection of arbitrary code.
4. Where a user is unauthorized to enter.

Independent ☒ Negotiable ☒ Valuable ☒ Estimable ☒ Small ☒ Testable ☒

Definition of done: the tests and analyses have been carried out, and it was proven that the app challenges users when attempting to access the above-mentioned areas, and the app did not crash or freeze during the tests.

Definition of done achieved ☐

Security User Story ID # 016	Missing Authorization	Secure Agile
Priority **2**	Story Points 1	

As a: **website or app user, stakeholder or data owner,**
I want: **privileges and rights to be given to users that are specific to their role only.**
So that: **sensitive information's confidentiality, location and integrity cannot be compromised, and functionality accessed that would lead to any number of vulnerabilities being realized.**

Test Steps and Acceptance Criteria

Manual Analysis.

(1) Perform a manual static analysis and assess the code for random or unrestricted permissions to conduct any activity in any area of the app.

Functional Analysis.

(2) Perform a functional analysis and assess the app's security for random or unrestricted permissions to conduct any activity in any area of the app.

Acceptance Criteria:

When all areas of the app are navigated to, the app restricts a user's ability to:

1. Read sensitive information.
2. Modify sensitive information.
3. Move sensitive information.
4. Edit sensitive information.
5. Invoke functionality only restricted users would be able to.

Independent ☒ Negotiable ☒ Valuable ☒ Estimable ☒ Small ☒ Testable ☒

Definition of done: the tests and analyses have been carried out, and it was proven that the app properly restricts users' abilities to perform actions in the areas navigated to, and the app did not crash or freeze during the tests.

Definition of done achieved ☐

Security User Story ID # 017	Hard Coded Credentials	**Secure Agile**
Priority **2**	Story Points **1**	

As a: website or app user, stakeholder or data owner,

I want: to ensure passwords, keys, and other credentials are stored external to the code in a well-protected, strongly-encrypted configuration file or database, separated from external and local users of the same system.

So that: unauthorized users do not gain illicit access and perform unauthorized actions to include: compromising sensitive data's confidentiality, availability and integrity; learning the inbound authentication credentials, the outbound communication encryption, and the data-at-rest encryption.

Test Steps and Acceptance Criteria

Manual Analysis.
(1) Conduct a manual static source code analysis to assess for hardcoded credentials and references.
(2) Search the source code for common URL prefixes and suffixes such as: "http://", "ftp://", ".com", etc.
(3) The search should also look for common file path references such as: "/bin."
(4) The analysis must also seek clues for the use of user names and passwords, such as: ".username=egg_man" or ".password=mmt5371."

Automated Analysis.
(5) Conduct an automated static code analysis to assess for hardcoded credentials and references.
(6) Analyze the source code for common URL prefixes/suffixes such as: "http://", "ftp://", ".com", etc.
(7) The analysis must also look for common file path references such as: "/bin."

Functional Analysis.
(8) Conduct a functional test and in accordance with the purpose of the app, attempt to access databases, URLs, and other locations/functions, assessing if a user name/password challenge was made.
(9) With network monitoring equipment attached, assess for any data leaving the app that would indicate credentials were sent.

Acceptance Criteria:
1. There are no hardcoded credentials in the code such as URLs, user names, and passwords.
2. Challenges were made when access to restricted areas of the app were required.

Independent ☒ Negotiable ☒ Valuable ☒ Estimable ☒ Small ☒ Testable ☒

Definition of done: the tests and analyses have been carried out, and there were no hardcoded credentials in the app's code, including URLs, user names, passwords and locations, and the app did not crash or freeze during the tests.

Definition of done achieved ☐

Security User Story ID # 018	Sensitive Data Encryption	Secure Agile
Priority **2**	Story Points 1	

As a: **website or app user, stakeholder or data owner,**
I want: **all stored and transmitted data to be protected with strong, standard encryption.**
So that: **bad actors and unauthorized users cannot intercept, read or modify the data.**

Test Steps and Acceptance Criteria

Manual Analysis.

(1) Perform a manual static analysis of the app to determine if the app protects the confidentiality and integrity of transmitted and stored information. Look for evidence of strong, standard cryptology, and the use of VPNs.

Dynamic Analysis.

(2) Perform a dynamic analysis employing a network sniffer to determine if the app protects the confidentiality and integrity of the transmitted and stored information.

Functional Analysis/Attestation.

(3) With network monitoring equipment, observe the output and assess for any data leaving the app that would indicate transmitted data are not encrypted.

(4) If the tests in (1) and (2) are not possible, the product owner and development team should attest that organization-approved, strong, standard cryptography is employed.

Acceptance Criteria:

1. All stored data are encrypted using an organization-approved, strong and standard crypto module.
2. All transmitted data are encrypted using an organization-approved VPN.

Independent ☒ Negotiable ☒ Valuable ☒ Estimable ☒ Small ☒ Testable ☒

Definition of done: the tests and analyses have been carried out, and it was proven that all stored and transmitted data are encrypted using organization-approved, strong, standard crypto modules, VPNs, and the app did not crash or freeze during the tests.

Definition of done achieved ☐

Security User Story ID # 019	Untrusted Inputs: Security Decision	**Secure Agile**
Priority **2**	Story Points 1	

As a: website or app user, stakeholder or data owner,

I want: the app to employ integrity checking and bypass protection to protect against attackers modifying inputs such as form fields and cookies.

So that: authentication and authorization decisions are not made based on the values of inputs directly to the app, or from cookies and other external media that would lead to escalated privileges, the compromising of sensitive data, and the insertion and execution of arbitrary code.

Test Steps and Acceptance Criteria

Manual Analysis.

(1) Perform a manual, static code analysis to understand where any coding weaknesses may exist, based on the following (but not limited to) table of potential areas of untrusted ingress.

a.	Parameters and / or arguments	b.	URL components
c.	Cookies	d.	email
e.	Environment variables	f.	Databases
g.	Reverse DNS lookups	h.	Any external item providing the app data
i.	Query results	j.	API Calls
k.	Request headers	l.	Any input used for security decisions

Acceptance Criteria:

1. The app is not vulnerable to the above, (but not limited to) table of untrusted ingress points.

Independent☒Negotiable☒Valuable☒Estimable☒Small☒Testable☒

Definition of done: The app is not vulnerable to the above, (but not limited to) list of untrusted ingress points, and the app did not crash or freeze during the tests.

Definition of done achieved ☐

Security User Story ID # 020	Unnecessary Privileges	Secure Agile
Priority **2**	Story Points 1	

As a: website or app user, stakeholder or data owner,

I want: the app to prevent an attacker from gaining access to any resources enabled through privileges being granted that do not match the users' needs.

So that: unauthorized users do not: gain unnecessary privileges, execute any functionality or arbitrary code; compromise the confidentiality, integrity and availability of any sensitive data.

Test Steps and Acceptance Criteria

Manual Analysis.

(1) Perform a manual static analysis of the code and assess if it meets the following minimum requirements: the code runs using the lowest privileges needed to meet the app's purpose, certain tasks exist in isolation to reduce the escalation of privileges, authentication bypass vulnerabilities do not exist, and input validation is taking place on all user-input fields.

Functional Analysis.

(2) Perform a functional analysis by attempting to escalate privileges beyond what have been granted.

(3) Assess if authentication can be bypassed.

(4) Assess if the app rejects any improper input entered in user input fields.

Acceptance Criteria:

1. The code runs using the lowest privileges needed to meet the app's purpose.
2. Accounts for certain tasks exist in isolation.
3. No authentication bypass vulnerabilities exist.
4. Input validation takes place on all user-inputs.

Independent ☒ Negotiable ☒ Valuable ☒ Estimable ☒ Small ☒ Testable ☒

Definition of done: The app is not vulnerable to authentication bypass, privilege escalation, and the app did not crash or freeze during the tests.

Definition of done achieved ☐

Security User Story ID # 021	Incorrect Authorization	**Secure Agile**
Priority **2**	Story Points 1	

As a: website or app user, stakeholder or data owner,
I want: the app to perform authorization checks correctly.
So that: authorization mechanisms cannot be bypassed, unauthorized users and attackers do not gain access to resources they should not, sensitive information's confidentiality, integrity, and availability are not compromised.

Test Steps and Acceptance Criteria

Manual Analysis.

(1) Perform a manual static review of the code to assess if: user role mapping to certain data types and functionality exists, role-based access control to create and enforce roles at defined boundaries exists, the app properly provides permission to access data, based on the intended purpose of the app, access control mechanisms are enforced correctly on every page, sensitive pages are not cached (if a website), and access control lists, (if present) are set to the default 'deny all'.

Functional Analysis.

(2) Perform a functional analysis to assess if the app is able to properly assign the user to resources they are entitled to and that they are not granted access, functionality or resources beyond a previously determined level.

Acceptance Criteria:

The app:
1. Maps user roles with certain data types and functionality.
2. Possesses role-based access control to create and enforce roles at defined boundaries.
3. Properly provides permissions to data, based on the intended purpose of the app or its business logic.
4. Enforces access control mechanisms correctly on every page (if a website).
5. Does not cache sensitive pages (if a website).
6. Sets access control lists if present to the default 'deny all'.

Independent ☒ Negotiable ☒ Valuable ☒ Estimable ☒ Small ☒ Testable ☒

Definition of done: The app is not vulnerable to the above, list of minimum acceptance requirements, and the app did not crash or freeze during the tests.

Definition of done achieved ☐

Security User Story ID # 022	Critical Resource	Secure Agile
Priority **2**	Story Points 1	

As a: website or app user, stakeholder or data owner,

I want: to prevent security-critical resources such as data stores and configuration files being read or modified by unauthorized users.

So that: an unauthorized user will not gain access to sensitive information and compromise its confidentiality, integrity or availability, assume an identity and gain privileges within the app or system.

Test Steps and Acceptance Criteria

Manual Analysis.

(1) Perform a static analysis of the code to assess if such resources as files, shared memory, directories, APIs etc., have configurable permissions.

(2) Assess if the code contains library functions that modify permissions.

(3) Analyze function calls whose arguments hold the potential for malicious values.

Functional Analysis.

(4) Perform a functional analysis of the code to assess if the app is able to properly assign the user to resources they are entitled to, and that they are not granted access, functionality or resources beyond a previously determined level.

Acceptance Criteria:

1. Resources, such as files, shared memory, directories, APIs etc., have configurable permissions.
2. Library functions do not modify permissions.
3. Function call arguments do not contain malicious values.

Independent ☒ Negotiable ☒ Valuable ☒ Estimable ☒ Small ☒ Testable ☒

Definition of done: The app is not vulnerable to incorrectly configured permissions on files, APIs, modified functions, and function call arguments do not contain malicious script, and the app did not crash or freeze during the tests.

Definition of done achieved ☐

Security User Story ID # 023	Risky Cryptography	Secure Agile
Priority **2**	Story Points 1	

As a: **website or app user, stakeholder or data owner,**
I want: **the app to use standard, strong encryption algorithms for all data protection.**
So that: **attackers cannot break any non-standard or standard-but-weak encryption with relative ease, gaining access to sensitive material.**

Test Steps and Acceptance Criteria

Manual Analysis.
(1) Perform a manual, static code analysis to assess if the code uses strong, standard encryption or a trusted 3rd party encryption module for all encryption.
(2) Assess if the following cryptology schemes are not used: DES, SHA1, and MD4.

Automatic Analysis.
(3) Perform an automated static code analysis to assess if the following cryptology schemes are not used: DES, SHA1, and MD 4. Configure the testing tool appropriately to perform this particular test.

Dynamic Analysis.
(4) Perform a dynamic test to assess if any of the above, weak cryptography schemes are used.

Attestation
(5) If the above tests cannot be conducted, the product owner and development team must attest to the fact that strong, standard encryption is employed.

Acceptance Criteria:
The app:
1. Does not use weak algorithms such as: DES, SHA1, and MD4.
2. Uses strong, standard encryption or a trusted 3rd party module from an approved source.
3. Contains strong, standard encryption as attested to by the product owner.

Independent ☒ Negotiable ☒ Valuable ☒ Estimable ☒ Small ☒ Testable ☒

Definition of done: The app uses strong, standard encryption, and the app did not crash or freeze during the tests.
Definition of done achieved ☐

Security User Story ID # 024	Authentication Attempts	Secure Agile
Priority **2**	Story Points 1	

As a: **website or app user, stakeholder or data owner,**
I want: **the app to prevent attackers from constantly attempting access to the app or website.**
So that: **attackers cannot succeed with brute force attacks that maintain a persistent threat to the website or app in order to gain unauthorized access.**

Test Steps and Acceptance Criteria

Manual Analysis.

(1) Perform a static analysis to assess if the code possesses the ability to lock the user out after a pre-defined number of failed attempts, has additional authorization measures such as a captcha or timeouts to increase the interval between successive login attempts.

Dynamic Analysis.

(2) Perform a dynamic analysis using fuzz testers to assess the ability of the app to reject successive, failed authentication attempts.

Functional Analysis.

(3) Perform a functional test to assess if the app possesses the ability to lock the user out after a pre-defined number of failed attempts, has additional authorization measures such as a captcha or timeouts to increase the interval between successive login attempts.

Acceptance Criteria:

The app:

1. Locks a user out after a pre-defined number of failed attempts.
2. Applies additional authorization measures such as a captcha.
3. Imposes timeouts between successive, failed login attempts.

Independent ☒ Negotiable ☒ Valuable ☒ Estimable ☒ Small ☒ Testable ☒

Definition of done: The app uses multiple measures to prevent constant and sustained attempts at gaining access to an app or account, and the app did not crash or freeze during the tests.

Definition of done achieved ☐

Security User Story ID # 025	One-way Hash Salt	**Secure Agile**
Priority **2**	Story Points 1	

As a: **website or app user, stakeholder or data owner,**
I want: **to prevent attackers from pre-computing the hash values of passwords.**
So that: **attackers can be prevented from bypassing any protection mechanisms lacking salt that would allow them to gain privileges using brute force and rainbow table attack methods.**

Test Steps and Acceptance Criteria

Manual Analysis.

(1) Perform a static code analysis to assess if the app: contains code that will generate a random salt on each occasion a new password is administered, adds the salt to the plaintext password before hashing it, generates a different salt for each password generation procedure, and the hashing algorithm is a strong, standard hash.

Automatic Analysis.

(2) Perform an automatic static code analysis to assess if the app: contains code that will generate a random salt on each occasion a new password is administered, adds the salt to the plaintext password before hashing it, generates a different salt for each password generation procedure, and the hashing algorithm is a strong, standard hash.

Acceptance Criteria:

The code:

1. Generates a random salt on each occasion a new password is administered.
2. Adds the salt to the plaintext password before hashing it.
3. Generates a different salt for each password generation procedure.
4. Uses a strong, standard hashing algorithm.

Independent ☒ Negotiable ☒ Valuable ☒ Estimable ☒ Small ☒ Testable ☒

Definition of done: The app generates random salts for each new password that's added to the plaintext password, that uses a strong hashing algorithm, and the app did not crash or freeze during the tests.

Definition of done achieved ☐

Tables for use in your organization

Now that the reader has studied the 25 security user stories, they should be adopted by the organization and integrated into whatever security process exists. One way to integrate them is to compare and map them to security controls that are already used by the organization. If the organization does not have a software security initiative, it should consider starting one, and reading this book is a first step. The following tables included in this book are available to all registered users as a download to allow modification and completion.

1. Mapping of this book's 25 security user stories to an organization's internal ID scheme.
2. Security User Story Test & Acceptance Matrix.
3. Security User Story Backlog Grooming.
4. Security User Story Points and Priority Assignment.

The following is a description of each table:

Mapping of security user stories to organization ID

Each security user story maps to the SANS Top 25 vulnerabilities. This table shows that mapping, but also allows the organization to enter its own reference ID# in the event it uses security controls that relate to those in the tables, but with a different ID scheme.

Security User Story Test & Acceptance Matrix

As has been seen, each security user story has acceptance criteria used to determine if a security user story has been coded and implemented properly. This table allows the Agile team members and product owner to fill out the form accordingly for each sprint and security user story. The testing and completion section has the following legend:

Security User Story Backlog Grooming

This table has already been featured in Figure 2 earlier in the book. This table allows the product owner to prioritize the security user stories and determine which ones feature in which sprint. The product owner simply populates the grid with an "X" to indicate which security user story should occur in which sprint. Security user stories may be repeated and appear in several sprints because a new sprint may mean a new component is being created for which the same security user stories also apply.

Story Points and Priority Assignment Worksheet

This table allows the product owner to assign story points and priority to each security user story. It also accommodates the organization ID# for each security user story.

		Mapping of security user stories to organization ID
ID#	Org ID#	SANS Top 25 Vulnerability
006	SU-004 (a)	Example Vulnerability
001		Improper Neutralization of Special Elements used in an SQL Command ('SQL Injection')
002		Improper Neutralization of Special Elements used in an OS Command ('OS Command Inject')
003		Improper Neutralization of Input During Website Generation ('Cross-site Scripting')
004		Unrestricted Upload of File with Dangerous Type
005		Cross-Site Request Forgery (CSRF)
006		URL Redirection to Untrusted Site ('Open Redirect')
007		Buffer Copy without Checking Size of Input ('Classic Buffer Overflow')
008		Improper Limitation of a Pathname to a Restricted Directory ('Path Traversal')
009		Download of Code Without Integrity Check
010		Inclusion of Functionality from Untrusted Control Sphere
011		Use of Potentially Dangerous Function
012		Incorrect Calculation of Buffer Size
013		Uncontrolled Format String
014		Integer Overflow or Wraparound
015		Missing Authentication for Critical Function
016		Missing Authorization
017		Use of Hard-coded Credentials
018		Missing Encryption of Sensitive Data
019		Reliance on Untrusted Inputs in a Security Decision
020		Execution with Unnecessary Privileges
021		Incorrect Authorization
022		Incorrect Permission Assignment for Critical Resource
023		Use of a Broken or Risky Cryptographic Algorithm
024		Improper Restriction of Excessive Authentication Attempts
025		Use of a One-Way Hash without a Salt

Table 1: SANS Top 25 to security user story & organizational ID mapping.

\multicolumn{2}{c}{Security User Story Test & Acceptance Matrix}								
App:		**Sprint #**	\multicolumn{3}{c}{**Scrum Master:**}			**Product Owner:**
\multicolumn{2}{c}{**User Stories**}	**Vulnerability**	\multicolumn{3}{c}{Tests}		\multicolumn{1}{c}{Completion}	**Security Lead:**
ID#	**Org**		**M**	**A**	**D**	**F**	**AC**	**DD**	**Notes**

ID#	Org	Vulnerability	M	A	D	F	AC	DD	Notes
000		*Example vulnerability*	X		X	X	*1,2,4*	*Yes*	*Auto scan had no false positives*
001		SQL injection							
002		OS Injection							
003		Cross-site Scripting							
004		Dangerous file upload							
005		CSRF							
006		Open Redirect							
007		Buffer Overflow							
008		Path Traversal							
009		Download Integrity Check							
010		Control Sphere							
011		Dangerous Function							
012		Buffer Size							
013		Format String							
014		Integer Overflow							
015		Critical Function Auth.							
016		Missing Authorization							
017		Hard-coded Credentials							
018		Sens. Data Encryption							
019		Untrusted Inputs							
020		Unnecessary Privileges							
021		Incorrect Authorization							
022		Critical Resource							
023		Risky Cryptography							
024		Authorization Attempts							
025		One-Way Hash Salt							

Table 2: Security user story test & acceptance matrix.

Legend:
- M = Manual Analysis
- A = Automated Analysis
- D = Dynamic Analysis
- F= Functional Analysis
- AC = Acceptance Criteria
- DD = Definition of Done

Security User Story Backlog Grooming																
Scrum M:		Product Owner:		Sprint Number												
App:		Security Lead:														
ID#	Org ID#	Vulnerability	1	2	3	4	5	6	7	8	9	10	11	12	13	14
000	SEC-004	Example Vulnerability	X								X					
001		SQL Command injection														
002		OS Command Injection														
003		Cross-site Scripting														
004		Dangerous file upload														
005		CSRF														
006		Open Redirect														
007		Classic Buffer Overflow														
008		Path Traversal														
009		Download integrity Check														
010		Control Sphere														
011		Dangerous Function														
012		Buffer Size														
013		Format String														
014		Integer Overflow														
015		Critical Function Auth.														
016		Missing Authorization														
017		Hard-coded Credentials														
018		Sensitive Data Encryption														
019		Untrusted Inputs														
020		Unnecessary Privileges														
021		Incorrect Authorization														
022		Critical Resource														
023		Risky Cryptography														
024		Authentication Attempts														
025		One-Way Hash Salt														

Table 3: Security user stories- backlog grooming.

Story Points and Priority Assignment Worksheet				
Sprint #			**Product owner:**	
ID#	**Org ID#**	**Vulnerability**	**SP**	**Priority**
000	*SEC-004*	*Example Vulnerability*	*2*	*1*
001		SQL Command injection		
002		OS Command Injection		
003		Cross-site Scripting		
004		Dangerous file upload		
005		CSRF		
006		Open Redirect		
007		Classic Buffer Overflow		
008		Path Traversal		
009		Download integrity Check		
010		Control Sphere		
011		Dangerous Function		
012		Buffer Size		
013		Format String		
014		Integer Overflow		
015		Critical Function Auth.		
016		Missing Authorization		
017		Hard-coded Credentials		
018		Sensitive Data Encryption		
019		Untrusted Inputs		
020		Unnecessary Privileges		
021		Incorrect Authorization		
022		Critical Resource		
023		Risky Cryptography		
024		Authentication Attempts		
025		One-Way Hash Salt		

Table 4: Security user stories: story points and priority assignment.

Registering, sign-up, and updates

Readers who register with the author will receive the following:

1. A soft copy of tables 1-4 in this book to allow modification, printing, and reuse
2. Any corrections and improvements made to this edition of the book
3. New, regular security user stories for subscribers to this service

Please send your name and contact email address to secure-agile@outlook.com. Registered users can also write to the author with questions and suggestions, as well as request customized versions of this book to suit their organization. Customized versions will include organizational logos on each page. The customized versions will only be available when sold in bulk to enterprises. Please write to the author to obtain bulk pricing and enterprise-wide licensing information for this book.

Useful Resources

SANS Institute

SANS is described as the most trusted and by far the largest source for information security training and security certification in the world. It also develops, maintains, and makes available at no cost the largest collection of research documents about various aspects of information security, and it operates the Internet's early warning system—the Internet Storm Center. The SANS Institute also created the 25 most dangerous software errors—the basis of this book—which are viewable at: https://www.sans.org/top25-software-errors/

MITRE

The MITRE Corporation is a not-for-profit company that operates multiple, federally funded research and development centers (FFRDCs). MITRE devised the very clever Common Weakness Enumeration (CWE) scheme that also aided in the development of the security stories in this book. CWEs provide a measurable set of software weaknesses that can be used by software security services and tools. MITRE maintains the CWE website with the support of the US Department of Homeland Security's National Cyber Security Division. Please visit: http://cwe.mitre.org/top25/

National Institute of Standards and Technology (NIST)

For IT, the National Institute of Standards and Technology accelerates the development and deployment of systems that are reliable, usable, interoperable, and secure. NIST advances measurement science through innovations in mathematics, statistics, and computer science; and conducts research to develop the measurements and standards infrastructure for emerging information technologies and applications. In particular, the Special Publication (SP) 800-53 is of interest to those in any area of IT security, and software security is no exception. This publication provides a catalog of security and privacy controls for federal information systems and organizations, and a process for selecting controls to protect organizational operations. The publication also describes how to develop specialized sets of controls, or overlays, tailored for specific types of missions/business functions, technologies, or environments of operation. Finally, the catalog of security controls addresses security from both a functionality perspective (the strength of security functions and mechanisms provided) and an assurance perspective (the measures of confidence in the implemented security capability).

For those who have never read SP 800-53, the author advises becoming comfortable with security user stories first, then downloading and reading SP 800-53, available here: http://nvlpubs.nist.gov/nistpubs/SpecialPublications/NIST.SP.800-53r4.pdf

Open Web Application Security Project (OWASP)

OWASP is a worldwide charitable organization focused on improving the security of software. Its mission is to make software security visible, so that individuals and organizations worldwide can make informed decisions about true software security risks. Everyone is free to participate in OWASP, and all materials are available under a free and open software license. Please visit www.owasp.org

About The Author

Stephen M. Dye is a software security professional who helps companies build secure software.

He applies multiple techniques such as threat modeling, secure code reviews, architectural analysis, and the built-in security measures featured in this book to enable a client's success. Stephen is also a mobility subject matter expert with experience in mobile apps, mobile device and mobile app managers. Stephen has authored several other books on GPS, machine-to-machine (M2M), and wireless instant messaging. He earned his bachelor's degree in electrical and electronic engineering from Bromley College of Technology in Kent, England, in 1987, and is C|EH, CompTIA Security+, ITIL V3, IC Agile, and Scrum Master certified. Stephen also earned the Honor Code Certificate for Cyber Security Technology, Application and Policy from the Massachusetts Institute of Technology.

Made in the USA
San Bernardino, CA
28 July 2016